All the Men I Never Married

This book is dedicated to my daughter, Ally.

All the Men I
Never Married

Kim Moore

Seren is the book imprint of
Poetry Wales Press Ltd.
Suite 6, 4 Derwen Road, Bridgend, Wales, CF31 1LH
www.serenbooks.com
facebook.com/SerenBooks
twitter@SerenBooks

The right of Kim Moore to be identified as
the author of this work has been asserted in accordance
with the Copyright, Designs and Patents Act, 1988.

© Kim Moore, 2021.

ISBN: 978-1-78172-641-9
ebook: 978-1-78172-642-6

A CIP record for this title is available from the British Library.

The publisher acknowledges the financial assistance of the Books Council of Wales.

Cover artwork: © Fred Tomaselli 2021.
Images courtesy of the artist and James Cohan, New York.

Printed in Bembo by Severn, Gloucester.

Contents

The past is magnified when it is no longer shrunk.
We make things bigger just by refusing to make things smaller.

Sara Ahmed

*How are we to represent, in writing, the fact that sexual desire lives
entangled with sexual violence? How are we to deal, in art, with
the powerful, destabilizing forces of both violence and desire?*

Katherine Angel

We are coming under cover of darkness,
with our strawberry marks, our familiars,
our third nipples, our ill-mannered bodies,
our childhoods spent hobbled like horses

where we were told to keep our legs closed,
where we sat in the light of a window and posed
and waited for the makers of the world
to tell us again how a woman is made.

We are arriving from the narrow places,
from the spaces we were given, with our curses
and our spells and our solitude, with our potions
we swallow to shrink us small as insects

or stretch us into giants, for yes, there are giants
amongst us, we must warn you. There will be riots,
we're carrying all that we know about silence
as we return from the forests and towers,

unmaking ourselves, stepping from the pages
of books, from the eye of the camera, from the cages
we built for each other, the frames of paintings,
from every place we were lost and afraid in.

We stand at the base of our own spines
and watch tree turn to bone and climb
each vertebra to crawl back into our minds,
we've been out of our minds all this time,

our bodies saying no, we were not born for this,
dragging the snare and the wire behind us.

1.

There was the boy I met on the park
who tasted of humbugs
and wore a mustard-yellow jumper

        and the kickboxer with beautiful long brown hair
            that he tied with a band at the nape of his neck

and the one who had a constant ear infection
      so I always sat on his left
        and the guy who worked in an office
           and could only afford to fill up his car
           with two pounds worth of petrol

and the trumpet player I loved
from the moment I saw him
      dancing to the Rolling Stones

        and the guy who smoked weed
        and got more and more paranoid
        whose fingers flickered and danced
        when he talked

and the one whose eyes were two pieces
of winter sky

and a music producer
long-legged and full of opinions

        and more trumpet players
           one who was too short and not him
           one who was too thin and not him

are you judging me yet, are you surprised?

Let me tell you of the ones I never kissed
      or who never kissed me

the trombonist I went drinking with
how we lay twice a week in each other's beds
      like two unlit candles

we were not for each other and in this we were wise
we were only moving through the world together for a time

there was a double bassist who stood behind me
and angled the body of his bass into mine
and shadowed my hands on its neck

and all I could feel
was heat from his skin

       and the lightest breath
            and even this might have been imagined

I want to say to them now
       though all we are to each other is ghosts
once you were all that I thought of

when I whisper your names
it isn't a curse or a spell or a blessing
       I'm not mourning your passing or calling you here

this is something harder
like walking alone
in the dusk and the leaves

       this is the naming of trees
            this is a series of flames
                 this is watching you all disappear.

2.

Many years ago, I lived in a house in the woods.
The woodcutter visited on nights when the moon
hid itself between the clouds.

Sometimes I go back to watch it happen again,
slip inside the body of the woodcutter,
to feel what it felt like to be him.

His arms and legs are heavier than mine.
The cigarettes on his heart, his lungs, his chest.
His finger to his lips, biting the nail to the quick.

I start to lose the border of where
his pain and mine begin and end.
I am in the body of the woodcutter.

But I am not *the* body of the woodcutter.
His body is a shallow dish and I'm a slick of water.
If I move too much, I'll spill out and over.

What I've really come back for is me,
ten years younger. Through his eyes,
she looks small and pale, a wisp of smoke

he could walk right through. Her face
turned in. Her mouth shut tight.
She smells of flight and all the things

this body hates. But when he presses her
to the ground, she vanishes inside herself
and nobody can reach her.

His tongue spits words I'd never say, and yet
here I am, inside his body saying them.
I leave the body of the woodcutter.

I leave it all behind – her, the house, the trees.
I return to myself, begin again.

Many years ago, I lived in a house in the woods.

3.

we walked into the beginning of summer and crossed a motorway to get to the woods / you didn't care about fences or gates / we thought nobody had ever been there / the smell was earth and rotting leaves / the only sound the distant singing of the motorway / we ate humbugs from a paper bag / you killed the wasps that came to sketch their way around us / we wanted something to happen / we were too young to know something was happening

we walked through the middle of summer and ran away from a man who pulled out his floppy dick / and waved it apologetically in our direction / we walked to your house / you hated reading and writing / you hated school / but you'd built a pigeon loft from a map in your head / trained birds to fall from the sky to your hands / you taught me about rollers / you taught me about spinners / you taught me / about the naming of birds / you held an egg up to the light / what was inside looked like a baby / some days I wasn't allowed to see you

we walked towards the end of summer and lay down in a field / we let the sun make its way across the sky / did I imagine the man on horseback watching / as we rolled around in sweet-smelling grass / which trapped the heat / which hid us from the world / which hid us from everything but the sky / maybe my heart made him up / maybe my mind made him up / we were young / we stayed still as if staying still meant he wouldn't see / we covered our faces / you held my head to your shoulder / when we looked again there was no horseman / there was only you and I / do you remember the horseman?

4.

his dad handing out shots
        bright green
liquid sloshing
over the rim
        onto my wrist
steam on the kitchen windows
and the living room
            full of bodies
      sitting in a circle
his mother nowhere
get em down
you Zulu warrior
          get em down
you Zulu chief chief chief
      follows me
the singing
      the dull thump of a bass
         the staircase bending
and swaying
      faraway bathroom
         my hand on the bannister
to keep myself here
      inside my body
         inside this house
      there's darkness to my left
there he is   on a bed
in the dark
         rolling a joint
          hey babe
I liked that word on his lips
      his friend
         at the open window
         letting smoke
slip out into the night
         it was good
to sit down

first I was there
      now I'm here

on the bed
　　　　on my back
　　　　　　　a naked woman
blu-tacked and glossy
stares down from above

then the weight of him
　　　　　　on top of me

at first it's funny
　　　　as I try to get up
his knees　　　　　　on my wrists
his hands　　　　　　on my shoulders
that panic　　　　　　in my belly
I'll remember it　　　　as long as I live

the friend coming towards me
　　　　　　a hand on my breast

the laughing　　　　　both of them laughing
my knee　　　　into his groin

he topples sideways

and I'm up and out of the room
and into the night

and the dark asks why
　　　　were you there in the dark
and the wind asks what
　　　　were you doing upstairs
and the moon asks why
　　　　were you wearing that skirt
but my body
　　　　my body asks nothing
just whispers
　　　　　　　see
I did not let you down I did not
let you down I did not let you down

5.

We hated the way you followed us around,
called us your girlfriends, the top of your head

barely reaching our shoulders, and the smell,
not just unwashed skin, the same clothes day after day,

the same trainers with holes in, but something else,
some animal smell I thought was contagious.

You often tried to hold our hands or stroke our hair,
or rest your small white fingers on our legs.

I wasn't sorry for you when we ran away
because you tried to lift our skirts above our waists,

or when the boys held their noses
because you'd peed yourself again.

It was Sports Day when one of the girls
finally snapped and hit you with a rounders bat.

I can still hear the thunk from across the field.
I wasn't sorry, even when you ran past crying.

At the other end of the track, children cheered
as the whistle was blown.

My friend said you'd tried to touch her bra-strap,
that she'd hit you again if she had to.

Brown sacks crumpled on the grass,
spoons from the egg-and-spoon race in a glittering heap,

children moving crab-like across the field
and you already running towards the classroom.

The next day your mother waited in reception.
She never came to parents' evenings or concerts,

yet there she was, hunched over and staring at the floor
while you sat next to her, pale-faced and silent.

I like to imagine I felt sorry for you then,
knowing you had nobody to speak for you about the bat,

your unwashed clothes, your hands,
the way they could not stop touching things.

6.

That a man approached you in a nightclub.
That you were polite at first, then turned your back.
That he insisted on giving you his number.
That you put it in your pocket.
That you danced with your friend all night.
That he stood and watched.
That you were drinking tequila.
That you licked salt from the back of your hand.
That he was waiting outside.
That he grabbed your arm and spun you round.
That you snapped.
That you've always had a temper.
That you were not afraid.
That you swung your fist and clipped his jaw.
That he kicked you between the legs.
That he shouted *I will end you.*
That you fell to the pavement.
That he tried to kick you again.
That a bouncer came and held him back.
That he shouted *I will end you, I will end you, I will end you.*
That the police were called.
That he vanished into the night.
That you were taken to the station.
That he turned up with his lawyer.
That he turned up with his father.
That you still hadn't sobered up.
That he was smirking.
That it was fresher's week.
That you were in pain.
That it was hard to explain about his number in your pocket.
That now you were afraid.
That you were advised not to press charges.
That you hit him first.
That this all happened many years ago.
That you laugh about it now.
That you say *well, I shouldn't have hit him.*
That I both agree and disagree with this statement.
That being our bodies in public is a dangerous thing.
That being in public is a dangerous thing.
That our bodies are dangerous things.

7.

Imagine you're me, you're fifteen, the summer of '95,
and you're following your sister onto the log flume,
where you'll sit between the legs of a stranger.
At the bottom of the drop when you've screamed
and been splashed by the water, when you're about
to stand up, clamber out, the man behind
reaches forward, and with the back of his knuckle
brushes a drop of water from your thigh.

To be touched like that, for the first time.
And you are not innocent, you're fifteen,
something in you likes that you were chosen.
It feels like power, though you were only
the one who was touched, who was acted upon.
To realise that someone can touch you
without asking, without speaking, without knowing
your name. Without anybody seeing.

You pretend that nothing has happened,
you turn it to nothing, you learn that nothing
is necessary armour you must carry with you,
it was nothing, you must have imagined it.
To be touched — and your parents waiting at the exit
and smiling as you come out of the dark
and the moment being hardly worth telling.
What am I saying? You're fifteen and he is a man.

Imagine being him on that rare day of summer,
the bulge of car keys makes it difficult to sit
so he gives them to a bored attendant
who chucks them in a box marked PROPERTY.
A girl balanced in the boat with hair to her waist
and he's close enough to smell the cream
lifting in waves from her skin, her legs stretched out,
and why should he tell himself no, hold himself back?

He reaches forward, brushes her thigh with a knuckle,
then gets up to go, rocking the boat as he leaves.
You don't remember his face or his clothes,

just the drop of water, perfectly formed on your thigh,
before it's lifted up and away by his finger.
You remember this lesson your whole life,
that sliver/shiver of time, that moment in the sun.
What am I saying? Nothing. Nothing happened.

8.

You must write, and read, as if your life depended on it…
                    Adrienne Rich

On the train a man asks me what I'm reading.
                    The mind as an empty and flooded field

He tells me about his job and his wife and his children.
                    The mind as water rising through green.

He tells me about money and Brexit and immigration.
                    The mind as a tree at the edge of the field.

I put my book away. Repeat. Repeat. I put my book away.
                    I have been putting my book away all my life.

I put away my hands and my mouth and my eyes.
                    I have been a long time without thinking.

I can sit here and listen and live without field or water or green.
                    I have been a long time without thoughts of my own.

Or go back and fold into myself.
                    White birds with no names.
                    They row away through the air.

Or enter and drink at the shallow place.
                    Enter and prepare to be followed.

I am worried about madness and the next sixty seconds.
                    I put away my heart and the stillness inside.

I smile and say what do you do tell me again and
how many kids do you have remind me again of your wife.

9.

Nothing has changed you still live with your gran
in a village where the lawns are edged with garden gnomes
it's a ten-minute walk to the canal which is so full
of water today I could reach over and stroke
its back so full another day's rain and it will be up
and over the sides how many years are you going
to show me your initials carved on the bridge
how many times will you tell me about the day
you were thrown into the water I no longer get
that clutch of fear at my throat when I think
of how you could have died before I met you
you are telling me again of how you toy
with the idea of living on a boat and I want to say
go on then do it or don't do it but don't
talk about it as if it's exciting talking about it
don't keep telling me you're tired again
you're sad again did you know I can't remember
your bedroom did you know this is the first time
I haven't wanted to touch your arm
for old times' sake remember one year
you helped me over the stile and left your hand
a second too long on my waist and I felt it again
the dizziness like vertigo but less dramatic
now you're telling me your ambition
is to get a twenty-two-year-old girlfriend
like your brother who has a problem with drink
and keeping a house clean but manages
you tell me to get a beautiful girl
or a *pretty little thing* as you call her
to sit on his knee and be all over him
I want to say do you ever wake up and worry
about becoming a cliché but I don't I can't
be bothered to keep being disappointed in you
and the way your beautiful animal face turned out

10.

two hours with you   sitting at opposite ends
    of your single bed

living the dream you say
    I can't tell if this is sarcasm

your feet level   with my chest
my feet level   with your waist

    almost like   being a teenager again
    almost like   a giving in

you put your hand on my ankle
    your eyes are closed

a train passes   the room shudders

the only thing speaking is your hand
    the slow circle of your thumb

I can't tell if you're dreaming
    or if this is something else

do we all have an ex we can't forget
not the one   that got away

but the one who left
not the one   who left for good

but the one that stays just out of reach
your thumb relearning the bone of my ankle

I know your patterns
    I know how this goes

maybe we have nothing left
    to talk about any more

can you feel my body humming
    underneath your fingers

do we all have someone we can't forgive?

11.

Once I knew a man who thought he knew everything. I often returned from work to find him asleep in my bed. It was like the sun had slipped itself between the sheets, or a lion, or something else born golden and sure of itself. Even though I knew all the stories about finding people in your bed, how it always ended badly – the three bears, the little girl with the red cape – what could I do but climb in beside him? He must have spent hours shaving his chest and back so that women like me could slide along him, as if we were bodies of water and he the dry and thirsty earth. The man who thought he knew everything never learnt that he didn't, and I realised too late. This was why he was the way he was, as if he'd been touched and turned to gold by a foolish, laughing king.

12.

After the reading a man waits around to tell me the poem I read about a beautiful man who thought he knew everything was objectifying men – how would it feel if the gender of the protagonist was reversed he says triumphantly – I reply that it would feel like most other love poems in the course of human history – he says aha! so this is really a very ordinary subject – I say yes if you discount subversion and poetic tradition and female desire – more accurately I only get to subversion and poetic tradition and female de… before he interrupts me to tell me how disappointed he is as I'm a better writer than this wasting my talent making cheap shots about men – the man in my poem does spend the whole poem naked so maybe he is a little bit objectified – but I like him that way – I start to write a poem about the opinionated man who is busy shaking his head at my misunderstanding of beautiful men and their complex desires which I've only skimmed over in my original poem by not giving my man a voice of his own – not allowing him to tell his own story – I'm about to make a general and sweeping statement about men when he interrupts again – isn't the man in your poem a bit one-dimensional he opines – can't you make him more interesting – just trying to be helpful he says holding his hands up like two little flags – like two dishcloths – like two dead moles hung on a fence – I reply no I can't – that is the best thing about him – or maybe I'm just wishing I said that – maybe I just smiled – nodded my head

13.

Although we've only just met, he's already telling me
that no, my suitcase isn't heavy at all, as he lifts it
with one hand into the boot.

He's not even reached the end of the road
and he's already telling me I have a crazy soul,
that he can tell how crazy I am.

He asks me do I know what he means, and I smile
and pretend that I don't. He says all the women
he knows who are artists or poets or musicians are crazy.

Crazy, crazy, crazy he says and I wish I'd told him
I was an accountant instead but on he goes,
taking his eyes off the road

to tell me all women who are artists are crazy in bed,
do I know what he means, they want to try
crazy things in the bedroom.

If he stops the car I could open the door and run
or pull out my phone and pretend someone is calling
or ask him politely what's wrong.

I could laugh at the next thing he says while the voice
in my head whispers that somehow I've led him on,
that I was asking for it.

I remember a train journey, everyone crammed in
and a stranger's penis pressed against my leg,
convincing myself

I was imagining it, or he couldn't help it,
where else in the place could he put it?
When we pull up at the airport

my arm flings open the door before I give it permission,
my left leg finds the pavement before I can think.
Still I turn back to give him a tip

and he's laughing, saying *relax, just relax*, and I know
that he knows I'm afraid, that I've been afraid all my life,
but it's not this that makes me ashamed.

14.

I imagine you at home on the other side of the world
in a town I don't know the name of, driving your wife mad,

leaving your laptop in the fridge as you go to get a beer.
It's hot. You're wearing shorts and a dark t-shirt.

Your white feet look like two fish washed up on a beach
and gasping their last breath. I know this although

I've not seen your feet in this life. The last time we met
you were fully clothed, black jacket, jeans, but now

without them, I can see you stand with a stoop,
your shoulders hunched, your body apologetic.

You are singing something I can't make out, your high
thin voice threads through the window and across

time zones and oceans to me here. When I think
of your voice, my soul drifts downwards inside my body

like a leaf falling side to side through the air.
Remember that night we were leaning into each other

like two doors loosening from their hinges?
Remember the darkness and how we almost

held hands? It wasn't even that I wanted to.
But I didn't not want to. It was complicated.

15.

I knew he was dangerous, that he had a girlfriend
he'd been with for years before he left her behind,
easy as slipping off a coat, knew that was a bad sign
but didn't know enough to keep my distance,
to not pick up the phone when his name appeared.
Oh I knew nothing back then, I thought sex was a promise
that would keep being fulfilled, I thought love was a knife
pressed to the throat, I thought there was a blade
in each of our hands. I am telling this now so he appears,
as real as that first night when we didn't sleep.
The slight red stubble of his beard, the freckles
covering his arms – his gaze, his attention all mine –
oh back then I never wanted it to end, the touching,
the looking, I didn't know that a person is already fractured
by the time that we meet them. It was just like Rilke said,
his gaze was a lamp turned low, although in those days
I knew nothing about what it was to be seen, what it means
to change or be changed, to appear, to burst like a star.

16.

When you rewind what happened, your fist
moving away from my face, your arm pulling back,
tracing a half moon in the air, do you watch yourself
running backwards from the flat,
that moment and all of its violence unfrozen,
do you imagine me rising from the bed,
the look on my face before I answer the door?
Do your words return and push themselves back
into your mouth, are you forced to swallow them
again and again? Not *sorry* but *you fucking bitch*,
those words and ones like them, finally lifting from my skin.

I know the living can haunt the living without trying.
Slag. Slut. If I imagine our lives in reverse,
my eyes are always lifting from the floor,
good things are happening. Are you watching
as I vanish into the last gasp of a bus,
reversing through the city? Sometimes I imagine
seeing you again, back row of chairs at an event,
your arms folded, listening to me read
about transformation and violence and loss.
You cannot touch me when I'm speaking,
though what I'm speaking about is us.

17.

One of my exes shared my poem on Facebook
and wrote *I'm glad you didn't write one about me*
and I replied *how do you know I didn't write one about you*

and he wrote back *because only the women in my family*
know the real me so I replied *I think you've misunderstood*
what a poem is for then he wrote *ok I'll let you win this one*

just like you won my heart (poem) which pissed me off
because of his use of brackets. Also, there was no winning
of hearts. Once I saw him sniff cocaine

from a toilet seat in the ladies' loo and when he turned
and looked back at me his eyes were bright
like crushed flowers left inside a book.

I never saw him cry or get angry or shout.
I made him laugh but couldn't tell you what it felt like.
I never borrowed one of his shirts and forgot to give it back,

although there were nights I wore his boxer shorts to bed.
I saw him lots with no clothes on but loved best seeing him
in just his jeans, the way they hung from his hips,

the bones jutting out like two beautiful half-formed wings.
On our first date we went to an art gallery and I hated him
for it because I didn't know what to do.

Once we walked to town and he kept asking over and over
why the cranes all point the same way and I said I didn't know
and he said well think about it logically and I kept saying

I don't know. I knew if I started one thought in my head
about those cranes or uttered one word
I'd never look him in the eye again and there'd be some sort

of permanent damage to my heart. Now I have to tell him
I wrote a poem about him, but at least I can say
you were right, I didn't know you, I didn't know you at all.

18.

This is not love. We are not speaking of love.
We are singing of Hardy: *Woman much missed,*
how you call to me, call to me – we are speaking
only of this. Outside I shout the whole thing

into the wind. There is darkness between us,
there is the ocean. My lips are moving
but nothing is heard. This is not love but it is
something like it. Here we are with the loyalty

of clouds. We are drifting, two boats on the water.
You have the wild in you, little wolf.
This is what happens when the body is a boat
and the heart is high and bright as a lantern.

19.

Your job was drinking. It was
the chore you assigned yourself
each night, a few cans with us
then taking three or four to bed
while you listened to music
on your headphones.

You drank steadily and well
and if we ever remarked
on the crushed cans pressed
like black and golden flowers
beneath your bed, it was never
in your hearing.

Eventually you moved out,
got yourself a flat, and so
the last time I saw you it was summer.
You were sunbathing on the slag bank,
your chest and arms covered
in an angry rash.

I knew it was you because of the cans,
scattered like spoor around your tent.
I didn't recognize your eyes,
the way you moved.
You'd been sleeping outside for days,
told me the stars were beautiful up here.

Here, you'd say, reaching out
to almost touch me on the arm,
ready to launch into another
of your stories about your neighbour
or someone you'd met
on the street.

Here, you say, speaking now
though you're long gone, stretching out
the word so it becomes two syllables –
Ee aar, moving forward on your chair,
repeating the word over and over
until I turn to you, and listen.

20.

It's just me and him, alone in the staffroom
and he's talking about a colleague he hates.

I bet she has a big pubic mound. I bet
it's covered in spider's legs.

He's already on about the next thing wrong
with his life, his job, with this woman.

I'm thinking about the women I know,
how good they are at getting rid of things,

experts in the endurance of pain.
Look at me now for example, sitting here

not moving a muscle as I remember
taking a razor to my upper lip

because the boys at school called me names.
My mum saying *what have you done?*

You're too young for all this. Once you start
you can't stop, there's no going back.

After that there was bleach, the flame of it
on my skin, testing myself –

how long could I stand it, how much
could I make disappear.

Then electrolysis, a needle into each follicle
and one dark hair at a time wished away.

Back in the staffroom he's saying
the next time someone annoys me

I should *flash them my tits,*
miming the action while making a cuppa.

Milk, no sugar, I say with a smile
I hate myself for. I remember all the times

I heard that as a teenager. *Get your tits out
for the lads.* It sounds obscene now

but back then it was nothing, just one
of the things that boys said.

In my first class of the morning
a boy asks why I have hair on my lip.

My stomach still drops like it used to
but I answer calmly this time.

All women do. Your mum probably does.
He looks outraged, maybe doesn't believe me

and how can I blame him?
This is not what they told him

about bodies and women
and I long for the staffroom

and the easy misogyny
and the laughing along with it all.

21.

When he tells me I'm not allowed to play with cars
because I'm a girl, I bring his arm up to my mouth
and bite. I'm sent to the Wendy House to pretend

to be good. Blank-faced dolls stare up at me.
Pretend oven filled with plastic fish-fingers.
Pretend windows with flowery curtains

sewn by someone else's mother. Pretend hoover,
pretend washing machine. Pretend teapots
and tea-set. I watch through a gap in the wall

as my teacher sits in her chair, crossing her legs
in the way she told us only yesterday
we should copy. *Be ladylike* she said.

Stop showing your knickers. I'm burning in here
as she calls the class to order, waits for them
to cross their legs and settle. I long to sit

at her feet, listen to all the old stories
of sleeping women who wait to be rescued.
The book is a bird, its wings held tight in her hands.

She bends the cover back so the spine cracks,
balances it on one palm, turns to me and tells me
turn around, at once, face the wall.

22.

That night, which I knew would be the last night,
when I said *be straight with me* and you kissed me again,
when I said *I think I'm more into this than you are*
and you kissed me again and said *let's go back to bed.*
Afterwards I said *answer me*, the night and the morning
still lodged in my chest, my body turning under your hands
as you said *yes, I guess you probably are* and then I knew
I could not fall into the body place with you again.
That the body can want one thing and the heart another,
that the heart can already be moving on
while the body yearns for the familiar embrace once again.
These were the things I learnt from your face,
tracing the outline of your bones and the slickness
of your chest. In the day you put on a suit and tie
and caught a train to another place. I ran with you
in the wind and rain, on the track or at the beach
and we thought nobody knew we went home together.
You did your washing on a Sunday and folded your clothes
and ironed your shirts and nothing could change this routine.
You were full of ambition for yourself and disdain
for your students. But in the dark you were none of this,
you were heat and blood and fingers and chest,
there was nothing neat about you.
Where are you now, did you get to London like you wanted,
are you in another immaculate flat, do you still read the papers
at the weekend, is everything tucked in, put away?
Part of me still hovers there, trying to work out
how you managed it, to hold something back,
how I managed it.

23.

It didn't really help, the story of Othello and Desdemona
and Iago and poison in the ear and though our teacher

taught us about poor Desdemona, bad Iago, Othello escaped
almost blame free, possessed by jealousy, driven into a state

so when my ex became my stalker all the boys in class ignored me
and every lesson he looked through me until the evenings when he

was drunk and in a nightclub and then he'd ring and start to cry
and try to find out where I was or where I'd been, asking why

I wouldn't listen, why I'd stopped picking up the phone.
Sometimes I answered it with silence, imagined him alone

listening to my nothing. That year of A-Levels, I got myself a stalker
and the police said *aren't you flattered?* In the station there was laughter

at the forty phone calls every day for weeks. He said that I'd agreed to
be with him forever, and then I'd changed my mind, what could he do

but become my stalker and wait till darkness fell and slash my father's tyres
or call fire engines to my house though there was nothing catching fire.

When my ex became my stalker, he convinced my mum to let him in
then locked himself inside the bathroom. It felt like I'd let him win

even though it finished with him in a police cell because of texts
he'd sent with threats and words like *kill* and *guess what happens next*

and so the police kept him overnight to think about his actions
and rang his mother who had no idea how any of this happened.

24.

She told me that when she woke, she was in the dark
in a strange room, fully clothed, apart from her knickers,
which she never saw again, apart from her top and bra,
pushed up round her throat. Imagine waking into silence,

to strange shapes in the dark, not knowing if you're alone.
Her shoes still on her feet. Her feet still in her shoes
and something deep inside aching, and nothing to do
except stumble from that bed and run away,

nothing to do but pass down the hallway like a ghost.
Like a ghost, disturbing nothing, holding her breath
until she was out in the crispness of a November morning,
walking along an avenue of silent trees.

She told me she remembered standing at a bar
and a hand in the small of her back that felt like fire.
The world slowly turning and her at the centre,
no ghost yet, but getting smaller.

And she remembers a hand loosening a tie
but not what happened after. Nothing about a face.
Her body no longer hers. And somewhere is the man
who did this to her. And somewhere is the man

who must have put her in that bed and walked
that same avenue of trees, waiting for her to leave.
I learnt this when I was young, that these things
can happen, that it's possible to walk into a bar

one evening and wake up in a stranger's place
with someone's semen dried between your legs
and though your throat cannot remember saying no
your heart cannot remember saying yes.

25.

When I tell them about my body
        and all the things it knows
they tell me about their guilt

they flourish their guilt
        as if they are matadors
in a city where people love blood

or they wave their guilt at me
        as if it is a flag of a newly formed country
and they are proud to be its citizens

sometimes they hold their guilt in their right hand
        and fan it out
like a deck of cards in a high-stakes game

or open up their guilt as if it is a book
        in a foreign language
they cannot understand

one held the two corners of his guilt
        as if it was a bedsheet
he must spread over my body

as if my body was a chair
        in a house closed up for the winter
and when he walked away

he left his guilt behind
        I run my hands along each edge
turns out his guilt is very small

not like a sheet at all
        more like a handkerchief
I shout have you forgotten something

but he is walking away whistling
        so I put it in my pocket
carry it with me always

26.

Once I went on what he called a date
and I called driving around in his car
which had one of those exhausts
that roared and made people turn
and look as we drove down the street.

The more we drove the more I realised
his personality didn't really suit the car
or maybe it did, maybe that was the point.
I was also young and sometimes cruel
and because language had deserted him

I decided I also would not speak.
I was annoyed at not sitting in a pub
or eating a meal at a restaurant,
even more annoyed when he pulled up
outside McDonald's

so I made a vow of silence,
though I was perfectly capable of speaking;
though talking is something I enjoy,
but I was tired of being kind to men,
always making them feel better about themselves.

I sat like a stone in his car
or a fish he would never hold in his hands.
We watched the late-night swaggering
of seagulls as they waited for scraps
from groups of squealing teenagers

who were squashed into neighbouring cars
and clambering over each other like puppies.
It wasn't his fault I was far away
from all of that – how could he know
I'd lived with violence and survived?

I was only a shadow pretending
to be a woman in a car,
a stone pretending to be a woman
in the dark or like somebody returning
from a land nobody else could see,

though its borders were under their noses,
though its generals lived next door.
I can't remember how I got home
or how the awkward silence was broken.
I understood violence as something of love;

never from a stranger or acquaintance.
Years later he finds me online, sends a message:
Do you remember me? It's me, J__. I'm sorry
I was so immature back then. I want to explain
that I was a stone in the shape of a fish,

the bones of a fish trapped in a stone
but I know it doesn't make any sense.
God, I'm frightened for my daughter
and the risks she will take. I write back
no, you have nothing to apologise for.

27.

Each week you jumped up and down in frustration,
your grey hair flopping like a broken wing.

Once you threw the baton across the classroom
and hit the drummer in the eye.

At rehearsals you always wore the same faded jeans,
the same off-white trainers laced up tight

but at concerts appeared in shirts that billowed
as you moved, satin-white with red hearts

or blue with yellow polka dots. You said the outfits
were just to make us smile, distract us from our nerves.

I walk past a brass band playing carols and think of us
back then, those evenings playing under lampposts

in a pool of light – *Coventry Carol, In The Bleak Midwinter,*
Hark The Herald Angels Sing. One night it was so cold

all the valves froze solid, first the bass and euphonium,
then the baritones stopped speaking.

Like animals dying from thirst
they fell in order of size, tenor horns next,

then cornets one by one, and yours
the last to stop its song.

It's been years, but sometimes I repeat
your words without thinking.

Today, I too was moved to jump up and down
as my junior band slowed to a crawl.

I roll up my sleeves,
trace the same patterns in the air.

28.

Now that I'm with you, it's no effort at all
to remember the mornings I lay in your bed
as you played transcriptions of Chet Baker solos.
The slight tilt of your hips. The veins on your forearms
lit up from the strain. How you spent hours
erasing the movement in your face, so the high notes
came easy, like reaching out and taking them down
from a shelf. I'm following you into a basement bar.
Your trumpet is slung over your shoulder
and you're talking to me about gigging and loneliness
and a New York musician I'm pretending I've heard of
because this isn't my world any more.
I get along without you very well, of course I do.
Play that one to me now, like you used to.

29.

Once I knew a man who ran with the hounds. He would stand on a hill and watch the pack pass by, then imitate the Huntmaster's commands, calling the hounds to him and patting their heads, letting their tails thump against his legs. Sometimes he looped as many collars as he could around their necks then let them run, pulled along behind them like a kite. Other days he'd lay down in the heather and watch the clouds form and reform above his head, and tell the hounds the story of Actaeon, how he was ripped apart by his own dogs, how their teeth closed on the throat of a stag, but really it was their master's blood which filled their mouths and splashed across their chests. He told them the story of the last wolf, killed on Humphrey Head, told them this wolf was their brother, and not the grey enemy they'd been taught about. They listened to him gravely, their tongues lolling from their jaws, their great heads resting on their paws. When it was too dark to hunt, he took them back to the Huntmaster, still quartering the fell in his blue livery-coat, calling their names until his voice was a scratch on the sheet of the night. Then the man who ran with the hounds was happy, because there was one more flame of a fox still burning somewhere in the dark, but he was also sad, because the man who owned the hounds also owned the woods and the hills and the fields and all the things that moved through them and beneath them and though he vowed that he would never be owned, he knew the night would always be a slate with half of its story untold.

30.

On the way from A wing to B wing
two prisoners start to circle each other

on the long corridor they call the high street,
where the leaves gather in corners.

They push their foreheads against each other,
their arms thrown back behind them.

The wind whistles past the canteen,
past closed doors, through the high grilled windows.

A guard shoves me through a gate, a hand
in the small of my back, locks it after us.

We watch men emerge from cells
and gather round the two still locked together.

It's like an old black-and-white silent movie
except even the black is a washed-out grey –

their jumpers and jogging bottoms,
the doors a darker shade, the walls

an almost-white, and just those leaves,
bright spots of colour, stirring a little

before they settle, brittle enough
to turn to dust if I could touch them

and not a sound from the men watching
or the two who are swinging at each other.

The alarm shrieks and prisoners drop to the ground
like fallen trees and we turn away.

Our men are waiting in the prison library
with poems on scraps of paper in their pockets.

Today Matt is leaving and Jack reads a poem,
tells him to never come back, forget they exist,

and Joe smiles like he's forgotten how,
and Luke says it rains in his mind, all the time,

and Arjun tells us about a country
where battles were fought with poems instead of swords.

They are listening, some with their eyes closed,
their heads cradled in their arms,

some with their eyes wide open.
When the bell calls them back to cells

they walk out of the room and are transformed,
back to fallen trees, or they become the wall

and never leave, or they change into a scrawl
of barbed wire and no one ever touches them again,

or they become the bars of a locked gate
and cast their shadows on each other,

they become the silence, they become the corridor
and men walk up and down inside.

31.

*According to research from AI firm Sensity – 96% of deepfake videos are pornographic and used to target women**

I'm making this a #NotAllMen free zone
so let me tell you about a darkened room.
In bed he trawls for photographs to clone.
Our man seems bored – hums a wordless tune

whilst watching violence played out like a game,
arms and legs and heads moved up and down
by unseen hands. He thinks it's not the same
as real life, as going into town

to assault a stranger, not the same
as kidnap, rape or causing *actual* pain.
He's safe. He tells himself that these freeze-frames
he makes are art, that each day he abstains

from cutting someone up in real life
he needs a prize. His images are knives.

//

He needs a prize – his images are knives,
could cut the toughest skin. Since he began
with her, he's watched as others have joined in.
Her face held on these sites – it's a surprise

to him how fast it grows, how men enjoyed
the call to arms, that when he gave her name
they wanted to abuse her. She's to blame
he thinks, sends more photos into the void,

more lies about this woman that he longs for.
She stays intact despite the things he's done.
He tells himself it's just a bit of fun.
He tells the boys keep going, he wants more

although he knows it's getting out of hand.
He goes back slowly through her Instagram.

//

He goes back quickly through her Instagram,
reads her status updates, line by line.
It's almost like he's there in Amsterdam,
watching her drink a glass of sparkling wine.

He pastes a nameless body on top of hers,
puts countless images of her stolen face
through algorithms, decides that he prefers
it when she's faked and trapped in porn, debased.

He doesn't know I'm busy writing this,
pinning him inside this book, my deepfake
cut-out, included here inside this list
of all the men – a bad-man-villain-snake.

Is it wrong to say I find him boring?
Look – he hears the word is out. It's galling.

//

Then he hears the word is out. It's galling
how he's talked about, but no one knows
his name. People say things like *appalling*,
what a scumbag. Maybe now she'll close

her social media, just disappear.
The police told her it's all a waste of time,
it's not revenge pornography. They're clear –
nothing he's done is counted as a crime.

Still, he's fading like a puff of smoke,
like fog in winter air. Of course it's fine,
he tells himself, she needs to take a joke.
She's campaigning to make his crime a crime.

He speaks up, says men should break their silence,
but thinks it's bullshit. It isn't really violence.

//

He thinks it's bullshit, it isn't really violence,
performs solidarity, enjoys
the gratitude of women, says he'll destroy
any man he catches – *call an ambulance*

for the bastards! He gets fifty likes
within the hour, though some bitch points out
his language *isn't helping*, it's not about
him or his *male posturing*. He types

fuck off, but then deletes and spits, puts down
his phone, thinks of her, being done to, taken.
He types the victim must be *angry, shaken,*
tweets his sadness with an emoji frown.

He's not broken any fucking law.
He doesn't know what she's crying for.

//

He doesn't know what she's crying for
and I don't know what men like him are thinking
and this is just a thing I try – the door
swings open – he turns around – he's blinking

in the sudden light. Or he stays hunched
and full of rage. There's too much I don't know
about his life – does he meet friends for lunch,
does he have a family? Maybe I should let it go,

this impulse to find out what makes him tick.
Did you hear about the man who made
an app that takes women's photos and strips
their clothes away? Turns out that I'm afraid

there's too many of these clowns, a medley
of strangers, colleagues, friends. Are you ready?

//

Strangers, colleagues, friends – are you ready
to learn who sees it as a free-for-all,
who's just watching, just downloading, friendly
but thinks it's just a bit of fun. It falls

the wrong side of revenge, not quite assault,
flirts with stalking, squeezes past harassment
but will not fit inside a police report.
If this was a story, an enchantment

would be created by these seven goes
at fourteen lines and all the men who did
these things would vanish or repent or show
they get it. You might feel implicated

if you're a man. I'm casting this in stone.
I'm making this a #NotAllMen free zone.

//

32.

You lived there for a week, in a country
you will not give a name to, not because
of what happened there, but because
you do not want this story to be changed
into a story of a country, you want it to be
the story of a man, or one-night-of-a-man,
a story of a hotel, or maybe the story of a lift,
the faded carpet, mirrors on every wall,
and his insistence, standing too close
and smiling, both of you pretending
you're good friends, maybe this is the story
of the corridor, how he asked you
where your room was, and you, stupid,
stupid, said down there and even pointed
and maybe this translated to follow me
to the room with birds fluttering behind
the walls, the room with birds living
between the walls, the room of curtains,
heavy, floor-length, blocking all the light,
the corners where nobody cleaned,
dust and the dead battery of a wasp,
you said my room is down there and then
kept walking, put your key in the lock
and he was right behind you, you felt
his breath on your neck so you turned
and put your hand on his chest
which may have looked like an invitation
except you were pushing, pushing him back,
who knows if you said no or if you said
I want to go to sleep or if you said both
but when you backed through the door
and slammed it closed, you remember it felt rude
to shut a door like that, so close to his face,
your heart beating in your chest
as if you'd been running very fast,
you remember thinking you were lucky,
luck got you out of it again, you sank
to your knees in the room of the birds,
you told yourself it was nothing

though it felt like something very bad
had almost happened, you swore
this would never happen to you
in silence and stillness again.

33.

I knew him when the summer was heavy with bees
and all the flying things were thrumming in the heat.

I walked with him once through How Tun woods
to find the path the foxes take, and yes I saw the marks

upon his arms, though I never heard him speak of pain.
I heard about the way he cut the steps into the slope

and strung lights from tree to tree to call the shadows in
and though I didn't see him dig the firepit, and only sat

with him beside its flames, I carried its breath
inside my chest and afterwards nothing was the same.

Later when they came to gather in the lights and cover
everything with earth, I thought I saw him through the trees.

I never slept inside his tent but not because I was afraid.
He stayed until the long rains came. I did not know his name.

34.

I clip the mic to the bell of my trumpet   set my shoulders
into a frame   that will hold the trumpet steady   hold it true
    take a breath   draw myself into my body   I am still
(like sand coming to rest in a glass of water)   nobody taught me this

    no man could put this into language   not my teacher
arriving for lessons on his motorbike   long hair streaming behind
    (unheard of where I was from)   a man with a hair bobble
just imagine   he taught me the word *gig*   I didn't know what it was

    thought it was something like a *jig*   some grand adventure
he taught me many things   how to be always on the road   rushing
    between one thing and another   my first paid gig
at the Haymarket Theatre   he taught me to watch the conductor

    to mark up the parts with cues   run to the bar and save his place
said *if in doubt blast it out*   and *no such thing as an uncertain trumpet*
    that you could do something you loved and live   that this life
though not lifting-carrying-wiping-cleaning   that this life was work

35.

You are telling me about the city, about the city starving,
about the siege and forgive me for only half-listening,

until you mention the woman with the cigarette
held between her fingers then quick between her lips,

how she stubbed each one out again and again,
her hair covering her shoulders. Forgive me for thinking

of her face when you're talking about the city,
about the city starving, forgive me for concentrating

on her skin, the woman with the nervous smile,
the woman with the sibilant name. All I can imagine

is her hair covering her shoulders, while outside
your city dwindled to nothing, forgive me for not asking

how you survived in there. It's true that at first
I was distracted by your eyes until you mentioned

the woman then she bloomed in my mind,
her bare shoulders, her long hair and now I know

something is ending when you say make love
and I say sex, but either way I realise I don't want to,

or more accurately I don't want to stop wanting it,
I'd rather stay here, poised on this edge with you,

neither one thing or the other, a beautiful balancing trick,
half-knowing nothing, half-knowing your body,

and please carry on looking at me in that way,
I feel unclothed when you do, just for you,

though not nude, but naked with you in this space.
But don't assume I'm the woman in that place.

If I'm anything, I'm the cigarette, burning.
And you are the city. And you are starving.

36.

he did not come to me as a swan
    or a shower of gold

        he was never a white bull
    the sort to lure you away from home

he was just a man
    like and unlike any other

        he stood by my bed in the dark
            afterwards no wife turned up
to take revenge
    to transform me into a cow

no god or father scooped me up
    the way Apollo carried Paris

from the battlefield
(there was no battlefield)

I didn't know it would be me
    who carried him here

        didn't know about walking
            the length of the self

        how the self disappears
            how hard it would be

            after five ten fifteen years

37.

There's always a train leaving for another place.
There's always a missed connection. A tree on the line.
A bridge down. Somewhere else (not here) there is rain.
Somewhere else (not here) there is weeping.
In a place with no station, no platform.
In a house nobody enters or leaves.
It would take many days to get there.
It would involve many hours of walking.
It would mean making a map and retracing steps.
Many years ago I vaguely got on the wrong train.
I wilfully got on the wrong train. I was thinking.
I wasn't thinking. I knew about the weeping stranger.
I gave the order to take up the track. I gave the order
to stop the trains running. I kept the bricks of the bridge
in my house. They basked in front of the fire like cats.
Nobody knew they were there. We called it the broken bridge.
We called it the passing place. We called it nothing.
The weeping continues. I look out of the window
at the sky and the stars, anything but the bridge
with the missing pieces and the house with no windows
or doors. When I go back for the weeping stranger,
I will need to follow the sun. I will have to leap over
the gap in the bridge, or else bring the bricks on my back.
When I get to the house it will be about hands and forgiveness.
The weeping continues. It's been there for years.
Like tinnitus in late-night silence. I tend to the river
though the river looks after itself. I gave the orders
for the train to run in other parts, in other places.
Something like work must go on.

38.

The night I left home, walked away even though
he told me to come back, I caught a night bus
into the city. Around me were young women
wearing the clothes I used to wear,
bra-straps showing, bare-legged, lounging like cats.
Their laughter washed over me as the bus
staggered and heaved itself around corners.
I didn't move as they swayed and fell into each other.
Through the window I watched a man
skirt a puddle, his briefcase against his chest,
a strange and solitary dancer.
He looked at me, then looked away.
I wish I could say I stayed out all night,
had a life-changing encounter with someone
homeless and lonely and worse off than me,
or even that I'd sat in McDonald's,
drank cup after cup of lukewarm tea,
vowed never to go back to him again.
The truth: I was too afraid to stay out all night
because everything wild within me had gone.
I went to my sister's, though I knew
he would find me. The path in darkness
and the crunching of snails underfoot.
The many small deaths of that night.
His fist on the door, again and again.
Realising he would not leave, pretending to her
it would be ok, that this was an ordinary row.
Making myself go downstairs and get into his car.
And what happened next, and what came after,
I do not remember. I see the same things you do now.
Him walking down the path in his leather jacket.
Me following after. The back of my head. His smile
as he opens the car and mock bows me in.
My sister standing in the light of the porch,
her arms crossed, angry and silent.

39.

I told you touching   would spoil everything   we should have just
kept circling the river   we should have just kept talking   you said you
were surprised to find yourself in a poem   that you'd never been the
one written about before   suck it up buttercup   I could write about
you for hours   so I guess in some sense I'm encouraging you   look
here I go   and there you are   lurching into another one of my
poems   the men who stand at the edges of dancefloors   are called
lurks   according to my sister who knows about such things   you
don't have to reply   consider yourself silenced   o muse   it can be
like Chris Kraus in *I Love Dick*   except without the art history   or
the memoir   or the philosophy   I don't want anyone to guess who
you are after all   I could write poems to you   and pin them to the
fence of your house   except you are one of those male poets without a
permanent address or any bills   or any sense of responsibility   other
than to yourself and your own pleasure   also I've been meaning to speak
to you about your books   successful in terms of prizes   but I'm bored
of reading the word whore in them   and I question this as a literary
device anyway   I can't pin poems to your fence   not knowing where
your mum and dad live   no don't tell me   that will spoil everything

40.

Also my ex and that first morning I woke up with him,
wasting it going to work but returning two hours later
to find him still there, the fresh new joy of it.

Also the smell of sex in the room, taking my clothes off again,
thinking there would be many days like it,
thinking there might not be a day like this again.

Also that he likes it when I talk about him this way.
Also how he only rang when he'd had a drink.
Also I understood even then about drink,

the way it makes passing truths seem things
you cannot do without. Also I was a passing truth
to him. He was a passing truth to me.

Also sadness at never using the body in that way again.
Also remembering the times I was angry with him.
Midnight and he's throwing stones at my window.

I'm playing Beethoven's 5th to drown out his voice.
Also not understanding how it had come to this,
from the bed and those mornings,

the press of bodies and skin, to this,
him out in the dark wearing my nightie
with my name on his chest.

Also realising it was a child's nightie (bear, flowers)
and the shame of not knowing that till then.
Also his numerous requests for nudes which I ignored.

Also Polly, asking whether I'd heard of the valley of shit,
me wanting to answer, I know someone who lives in it,
honey. But maybe I misheard.

Maybe she said something else entirely.
Also Polly, asking did I know that magpies
are actually scared of shiny things?

And me remembering the strange gleam of him
and wanting to keep him where I could see him,
under my eye, in my bed, between my legs.

The loneliness inside my chest and growing.
Also he called me *miss graceful arms* once in a text.
Also that my friends hated him.

Also that I swore he would never set foot in my flat again.
Also that stairwell. Stairs leading up to the roof
and that day slanting through my life like the brightest light.

Also that I left quickly, unhooked myself,
left him recovering himself, pulling himself together.
No, none of these, it was a gathering. Gathering himself in.

41.

If I'm ever bored of monogamy,
I'll come and find you,
we'll go to bed and do

things we would not do
with any other (I won't name
them here.) I don't blame

you for asking, I blame
you for not asking sooner.
I used to think you were a user.

I thought I knew what a user
was. I thought it was just lust
but you were the best

at some things, the best
that I've known. How we pretended
none of it mattered! It's splendid

to look back on it now, it was splendid
to know you. If I'm ever bored of monogamy
I know who to turn to.

42.

Is it ▮ if your husband/boyfriend/friend did it, is it ▮ if you didn't say no/yes, if you were arguing/not speaking, is it ▮ if he spits in your face and you just want it to stop, is it ▮ if you can't even write it, is it ▮ if you can't even say it, if you opened your legs, if you didn't protest, if you stayed with him after, is it ▮ if you pretend nothing has happened, is it ▮ if you did it to distract him, to make him stop shouting, to make him stop swearing, to make him stop leaving, is it ▮ if you became grey, if some bright fish of desire went into hiding for years, is it ▮ if you were frightened, not for your life, but for your mind, is it ▮ if your mind was slipping away and doing it was the only thing that stopped the slipping, is it ▮ if you did it so you could sleep, is it ▮ if you did it to stand in for forgiveness, if you had hate in your heart when you did it, if you had lies in your chest, is it ▮ if you didn't mean it, if you can't remember what happened, is it still ▮ if you never told anyone, if you didn't think about it again, if you moved on, if you're ok now, if you're ok now, if you're ok now.

43.

When I open my ribs a dragon flies out
and when I open my mouth a sheep trots out
and when I open my eyes silverfish crawl out
and make for a place that's not mine.

When I open my fists two skylarks soar out
and when I open my legs a horse gallops out
and when I open my heart a wolf slips out
and watches from beneath the trees.

When I open my arms a hare jumps out
and when I show you my wrists a shadow cries out
and when I fall to my knees
a tiger stalks out and will not answer to me.

Now that the beasts that lived in my chest
have turned tail and fled, now that I'm open
and the sky has come in and left me
with nothing but space, now that I'm ready

to lie like a cross and wait for the ghost
of him to float clear away, will my wild things
come back, will the horse of my legs
and the dragon of my ribs, and the gentle sheep

which lived in my throat and the silverfish
of my eyes and the skylarks of my hands
and the wolf of my heart, will they all come back
and live here again, now that he's left,

now I've said the word whisper it rape,
now I've said the word whisper it shame,
will my true ones, my wild, my truth,
will my wild come back to me again?

44.

I saw him fall, but before I saw him fall,
I watched him dance along the pavement,
his feet trying to catch up with his body
before he hit the ground face first –
his right arm stretched out, his left
tucked underneath and then a terrible bubbling
sound at every breath. His eyes were closed.
I thought they might not open again.
His blood was staining the pavement.

All through the 999 call I kept my hand
on his shoulder, imagining I could somehow
keep him here, as the operator kept repeating,
you need to keep calm, you need to breathe,
you need to stop the bleeding.
I lifted his head to push my jumper underneath,
watched as the flow of blood slowed down
and then his right leg twitched a little,
one shoulder lifted

and I kept saying *please be still, be still,
the ambulance is coming.* I held his head
in my hands, I could see the dark shine
of his eye, the swelling of his cheekbone.
It was July, it was warm but he was shivering,
saying *I want to go home* in a sing-song voice,
his blood drying now on my hands,
picking out my fingerprints and still,
no ambulance, two hours passed

and neighbours came and went, his son
arrived but did not touch his father,
or kneel down or speak to him in any way.
I began to think I would be there forever,
in the shadow of the son and his silent anger,
that this was a punishment I'd somehow earned,
as Sisyphus was doomed to push the stone uphill
so I was cursed to sit here, holding a man's head,
his mind, staying with him, watching while he died.

45.

Remember that night we'd been out drinking
and on the way home heard raised voices,

saw a couple across the road, arguing, leaning
towards each other and then he slapped her,

once across the face, then turned and walked away.
She stood there for a while and then she followed,

down Rawlinson Street as the lights from passing cars
fell on her, then swept on by. We didn't call out

or phone the police. We didn't speak, not to her
or him or to each other. When we got home

we didn't talk about the woman in the denim skirt,
holding her white shoes by the straps.

It's not possible I saw her feet, yet I remember them,
the blackened soles from walking on the pavement,

the sore on the heel where the strap had rubbed
and raised a patch of red. We did not speak to her

and so we made her disappear, limping into the night,
trying to keep up with that man, who knew she'd follow

so did not turn around, hands thrust into his jeans,
front door key hot between his fingers.

46.

I let a man into my room because I couldn't bear
the thought of him with someone else.
Even though he wasn't, never had been,
never would be mine. I showed a man
into my room as if I was selling him the space.
I opened the door and let a shadow
follow me inside. I didn't turn on the light.
I turned on every light. I allowed a man
into my room and he was kind.
I let a man follow me to my room
and didn't close the door in time.
I let a man push past me through the door
and told myself I didn't really mind.
I let a man into my room which turned
into a lift and we were together then apart
then together then apart depending on
whether the door was open wide.
I let a man into my body and let him sleep
inside my room. I let him in, I let him in,
I said that he could do those things
but only in my mind. I let a man
into my room and took a vow of silence,
took a vow of there's no turning back,
because a mind is not for changing.
The men inside my room do not like leaving.
They think they know my name
but one of us is lying. I step across
the threshold. I follow them inside.
Once they're in, they're in.
I open then I close my eyes.

47.

All night a bird beats its wings
behind the wall. In the space between rooms
it has the quietest scream. (I realise I cannot live
without desire.) At first I think it's trapped
behind the wall. Is it another bird
that moves, that seems to fall and rise again?
I am hiding something
in the mirror. In the morning
I am searching for myself
but see a bird rising up behind my eyes.
I think about a girl with hair covering her face
and the bruise of her body and one person listening.
I think about what he said, about the need
to *throw a stone behind to catch the one ahead.*
The bird calls to me from between the walls.

The bird calls to me from between the walls
to *throw a stone behind to catch the one ahead.*
I think about what he said, about the need
and the bruise of her body and one person listening.
I think about a girl with hair covering her face
but see a bird rising up behind my eyes.
I am searching for myself
in the mirror, in the morning.
I am hiding something
that moves, that seems to fall and rise again
behind the wall. Is it another bird
without desire? At first I think it's trapped,
it has the quietest scream. I realise I cannot live
behind the wall, in the space between rooms.
All night a bird beats its wings.

48.

When he told me not to tell the story
of my mother's hair, I was obedient
for many years, until I saw the video
of wild horses in Patagonia,
tamed by increments over many days,
the gaucho calm and still when the horse
met his gaze, then shooing it
as it looks away, and so the horse learns
that only when it gives its whole attention
to this man will it ever feel peace again.

And of course my mother is not a horse,
she would never be fooled by such a trick,
but maybe the man who told me not to tell
is the gaucho, maybe once I was a horse,
to spend all these years listening to his voice.
He told me this was women's business,
that the world was not interested in such things.
He said listen to me read Eliot until you fall asleep
or until the red wine runs out, and so we did,
all of us who had gathered there to learn.

He stood in front of the curved window.
The bats criss-crossed the lawn.
He did not hold a book, or open his eyes
to see if we were there. The room took
his voice and gave it back to every corner.
It felt as if he whispered in my ear.

I have held my tongue for years.
My mother's hair. I did as I was told.
She sat for hours between my legs
as if she was the child, and I the mother.
I straightened her hair, every curl and kink,
dividing it into smaller and smaller sections.
The hiss of steam. The TV in the background.
My father elsewhere, and part of me still there,

part of me in the library with the man
who told me not to speak about such things.
The lawn. The drifting dusk. The bats.
My mother's hair. My hands. That house.
The shudder of a horse's flank.

Acknowledgements

Thank you to the editors of the following publications in which some of these poems have appeared: *Agenda, Ambit, English: Journal of the English Association, MAL Journal, Poem, Poetry Ireland Review, The Dark Horse, The Morning Star, The New Humanist, The New Statesman, The North, The Poetry Review, The Rialto, The White Review* and *Wild Court*. No. 47 won the 2021 Ledbury Poetry Competition. No. 40 won third prize in the 2021 *Mslexia* Poetry Competition. No. 27 was published in the Candlestick Press 'Christmas Lights: Ten Poems for Dark Winter Nights' edited by Katharine Towers.

The epigraph for No. 8 comes from *What Is Found There: Notebooks on Poetry and Politics* by Adrienne Rich. No. 15 references 'Archaic Torso of Apollo' by Rainer Maria Rilke, translated by Stephen Mitchel. No. 18 contains a line from Thomas Hardy's poem 'The Voice'. No. 28 contains a line from the song 'I Get Along Without You Very Well' composed by Hoagy Carmichael and performed by Chet Baker amongst others. The first poem 'We Are Coming' is inspired by *The Laugh of the Medusa* by Hélène Cixous. No. 29 and No. 33 were commissioned by the BBC for the 2020 Contains Strong Language Festival. The Deepfake Sonnets (No 31) are offered here in solidarity with the poet Helen Mort and all women whose images have been manipulated and abused through the use of deepfake technology.

Thank you to Manchester Metropolitan University for the award of a Vice Chancellor's Bursary and to my supervisors Dr Nikolai Duffy, Dr Angelica Michelis and Professor Michael Symmons Roberts for their support and feedback on this work.

Thank you to Amy Wack and the team at Seren. Thanks to the Dove Cottage Young Poets for the inspirational workshops and chance to write alongside you all. Thanks to Abeer Ameer, Jennifer Copley, John Foggin, Holly Hopkins, Martin Kratz, Helen Mort, Jacqueline Saphra, Clare Shaw, Greta Stoddart, David Tait and Pauline Yarwood and special thanks to the "Poety" club – Amanda Dalton, Katie Hale, Hannah Hodgson and Carola Luther. Your friendship, conversations and feedback have been invaluable to me throughout the writing of this book. And finally, thanks to my husband Chris – my first and best reader.